T0071002

# Bob Chilcott
# Anthems 1

*10 anthems for mixed voices*

MUSIC DEPARTMENT

OXFORD
UNIVERSITY PRESS

OXFORD
UNIVERSITY PRESS

Great Clarendon Street, Oxford OX2 6DP, England
198 Madison Avenue, New York, NY10016, USA

Oxford University Press is a department of the University of Oxford.
It furthers the University's aim of excellence in research, scholarship,
and education by publishing worldwide

Oxford is a registered trade mark of Oxford University Press
in the UK and in certain other countries

© Oxford University Press 2002

The moral rights of the author have been asserted
Database right Oxford University Press (maker)

This collection first published 2002

All rights reserved. No part of this publication may be reproduced,
stored in a retrieval system, or transmitted, in any form or by any means,
without the prior permission in writing of Oxford University Press,
or as expressly permitted by law. Enquiries concerning reproduction
outside the scope of the above should be sent to the Music Copyright
Department, Oxford University Press, at the address above

Permission to perform the works in this anthology in public
(except in the course of divine worship) should normally be obtained
from the Performing Right Society Ltd. (PRS), 29/33 Berners Street,
London W1T 3AB, or its affiliated Societies in each country throughout
the world, unless the owner or the occupier of the premises
being used holds a licence from the Society

Permission to make a recording must be obtained in advance
from the Mechanical Copyright Protection Society Ltd. (MCPS),
Elgar House, 41 Streatham High Road, London SW16 1ER,
or its affiliated Societies in each country throughout the world

20

ISBN 978-0-19-353089-8

Music origination by Barnes Music Engraving Ltd., East Sussex
Printed in Great Britain on acid-free paper by
Caligraving Ltd., Thetford, Norfolk.

# Contents


| | |
|---|---|
| And Thank Him Then | 4 |
| Be thou my vision | 8 |
| Even such is time | 15 |
| God so loved the world | 21 |
| If ye love me | 24 |
| Irish Blessing | 29 |
| Just as I am | 33 |
| Song (from *Jubilate*) | 39 |
| Sweet Prospect | 52 |
| Walk Softly | 61 |

*For Julian Elloway, on his retirement from Oxford University Press, December 2000*

# And Thank Him Then

Early 16th century

**BOB CHILCOTT**

This piece © Oxford University Press 2002
This collection © Oxford University Press 2002

Printed in Great Britain

OXFORD UNIVERSITY PRESS, MUSIC DEPARTMENT, GREAT CLARENDON STREET, OXFORD OX2 6DP
Photocopying this copyright material is ILLEGAL.

poco rit.
11
mf
God's pro-vi-dence for sus - te-nance it is for man;
mf
a tempo
15
mp
Then we al-ways to him give praise, and thank him then,
mp
18
and thank him then.
22
mp
Plea-sure it is to hear, i - wis, the
mp

25
birds sing; The deer in the dale, the
28
sheep in the vale, the corn spring - ing.
31
mf
poco rit.
God's pro - vi - dence for sus - te - nance it is for man;
mf
God's pro - vi - dence for sus - te - nance it is for man;
poco rit.
mf

35
a tempo
mp
Then we al - ways to him give praise, and thank him then,
mp
a tempo
mp
38
p
and thank him then, and
p
dim.
41
poco rit.
thank him then.
poco rit.
p
pp

*To the memory of William Chambers*

# Be thou my vision

Early Irish
tr. Mary Byrne (1880–1931)
versified Eleanor Hull (altered) (1860–1935)

**BOB CHILCOTT**

A version of this piece (BC43) with piano accompaniment is available separately (ISBN 0–19–343292–7).
An orchestral accompaniment is available for hire, scored for Fl., Ob., 2 Cl. in B♭, 2 Hn. in F, Harp, and Strings.

Music © Oxford University Press 2000 and 2002; words © Chatto & Windus from *The Poem Book of the Gael*. Photocopying this copyright material is ILLEGAL.

14
poco cresc.
mp
best thought in the day and the night, Both wak - ing and
poco cresc.
mp
18
più dolce
poco rit.
a tempo
p
sleep - ing, thy pre - sence my light.
più dolce
p
22
Be thou my
mp espress.
TUTTI
S.
A.
Be thou my vi - sion, O Lord of my
Be thou my
T.
B.
mp espress.
mp espress.

27
heart, Be all else but naught to me, save that thou
Be thou my
31
mp
cresc.
art; Be thou my best thought in the day and the
mp
Be thou my
cresc.
mp
cresc.
35
mf
più dolce
night, Both wak - ing and sleep - ing, thy pre - sence my
più dolce
mf
mf
più dolce

39
mp
poco più mosso
S./A. unis.
mf
light.
Be my
T./B. unis.
mf cantabile
mp
Be thou my wis - dom, be
poco più mosso
mp
mf
43
unis.
poco cresc.
wis - dom, be my word; Be with me, and
poco cresc.
thou my true word; Be thou ev - er with me, and
poco cresc.
47
unis.
mf cantabile
I with thee, Lord; Be thou my great Fa - ther, and
mf
unis.
I with thee, Lord; Be my
mf

51
cresc.
I thy true son; Be thou in me dwell - ing, and
cresc.
Fa - ther, I thy son; Be with me, and
cresc.
55
f
dim.
poco rit.
Tempo I
I with thee one.
f
dim.
poco rit.
Tempo I
f
dim.
p sost.
Man.
60
S.
OLO
SOPRANO SOLO
p espress.
Be thou and thou on - ly the
Ped.

65
first in my heart; O Sov - ereign of hea - ven, my
69
mp espress.
trea - sure thou art; O Sov - - - ereign of
Great heart of my own heart, what -
mp espress.
Great heart of my heart, what -
Great heart of
mp espress.
mp sost.
73
mf
hea - ven, Be my vi - sion, be my
mf
- ev - er be - fall, Still be thou my vi - sion,
mf
mf

77
f
dim.
vi - sion, be my vi - sion, my vi - sion,
be thou my vi - sion,
be thou my vi - sion, be thou, be thou my vi -
thou, be thou my
be thou my vi - - -
for rehearsal only
82
mp
p
rit.
più lento
O Ru - ler of all.
- sion,
vi - sion,
Ru - ler of all.
- sion,
mp

# Even such is time

Sir Walter Ralegh (?1554–1618)

BOB CHILCOTT

Also available separately: BC11; ISBN 0-19-343208-0
This piece may be sung as a companion to *Love* BC10.

© Oxford University Press 1994, 1996, and 2002. Photocopying this copyright material is ILLEGAL.

5
e - ven such is time, e - ven such is time,
time, e - ven such is time, e - ven such is
is time,
joys, and all we have,
7
e - ven such is time, e - ven such is time,
time, e - ven such is time, e - ven such is
e - ven such is
And pays us but with age and dust

9
pp
e - ven such is time, Who, in the dark and si - lent
time, Who, in the dark and si - lent
time, Who, in the dark and si - lent
Who, in the dark and si - lent
12
poco cresc.
grave, When we have wan - dered all our
grave, When we have wan - dered all our
grave, When we have wan - dered all our
grave, When we have wan - dered all our

14
sub. f
ways, Shuts up the sto - ry of___ our days, And from which
sub. f
ways, Shuts up the sto - ry of___ our days, And from which
sub. f
ways, Shuts up the sto - ry of___ our days, And from which
sub. f
ways, Shuts up the sto - ry of___ our days, And from which
sub. f
17
earth and grave___ and dust___ The Lord shall
earth and grave___ and dust___ The Lord shall
earth and grave___ and dust___ The Lord shall
earth and grave___ and dust___ The Lord shall

19
mf
raise me up I trust, the Lord shall
raise me up I trust,
raise me up I trust, I
raise me up I trust, I
22
SOPRANO SOLO
mp
The Lord shall raise me up,
dim. poco a poco al fine
raise me up, the Lord shall raise me up, the Lord shall
the Lord shall raise me up, the Lord shall raise me up,
trust, I trust, I
trust, I trust, I
dim. poco a poco

24
p
the Lord shall raise me up,
raise me up, the Lord shall raise me up, the Lord shall
the Lord shall raise me up, the Lord shall raise me up,
trust, I trust, I
trust, I trust, I
26
pp
poco rit.
the Lord shall raise me up.
poco rit.
pp
raise me up, the Lord shall raise me up I trust.
pp
the Lord shall raise me up, the Lord shall raise me up I trust.
pp
trust, I trust, I trust.
pp
trust, I trust, I trust.
poco rit.
pp

*Commissioned in memory of Dan and Pat Jacobson by Jeanne Jacobson Stephens and Gary Stephens for the Lovers Lane United Methodist Sanctuary Choir, Dallas, Texas*

# God so loved the world

John 3: 16

**BOB CHILCOTT**

Also available separately: BC29; ISBN 0-19-343276-5

© Oxford University Press 1999 and 2002. Photocopying this copyright material is ILLEGAL.

30
rit.
a tempo
SOPRANO SOLO
p espress.
God so loved, God so loved, so loved the
pp
life. God so loved the world, so loved the world.
pp
37
p
world. God so loved, God so loved the world,
pp
p cresc.
God so loved the world, so loved the world, that he
pp
p cresc.
44
p cresc.
that he gave his son that who-so be - liev-eth, be - liev-eth in
gave his on - ly be - got - ten son that who-so be - liev-eth, be - liev-eth in

51
mf
f
p
him, should not pe-rish but have ev-er-last-ing life, ev-er-last-ing,
mf
f
p
59
SOPRANO SOLO
p
dim.
ev-er-last-ing life, ev-er-
p
ev-er-last-ing, God so loved the world,
ev-er-last-ing life. God so
p
64
rit.
p
-last-ing life, God so loved the world.
pp
God so loved the world, so loved the world.
pp
loved the world, God so loved the world.

*For Mark Toews and the Lawrence Park Community Church Choir, Toronto*

# If ye love me

John 14: 15–17

**BOB CHILCOTT**

© Oxford University Press 2002. Photocopying this copyright material is ILLEGAL.

8
f
mp
Fa - ther, and he shall give you a - no - ther com - for -
Fa - ther, and he shall give you a - no - ther
Fa - ther, he, and he shall give you a - no - ther
Fa - ther, he shall give you a com - for -
11
SOPRANO 1
pp dolce
- ter.
If ye love me, ye love
SOPRANO 2
If ye love me, if ye love me,
com - for - ter.
If ye love me, if ye love me,
com - for - ter.
If ye love me, if ye love me,
- ter.
If ye love me, if ye love me,

15
me, ye love me, and I will
keep, O keep my com - mand - ments, and I will pray,
keep, O keep my com - mand - ments, and I, I will
keep, O keep, O keep my com-mand-ments, and I, I will
keep, O keep my com - mand - ments, and I will
18
pray, I will pray, and he shall give you a -
I will pray the Fa - ther, and he shall give you a -
pray, pray the Fa - ther, and he shall
pray, pray the Fa - ther, he, and he shall give
pray, pray the Fa - ther, he shall give

21
poco rit.
a tempo
p cresc.
-no - ther com - for - ter, that he may bide,
-no - ther com - for - ter, that he may bide,
give you a - no - ther com - for-ter, that he, that he may
you a - no - ther com - for-ter, that he may bide, that
you a com - for - ter, that he, that
24
SOPRANO 1 & 2
rit.
mf
that he may bide, that he may bide with you for e - ver,
bide, that he may bide, may bide with you for e - ver,
he may bide, that he may bide with you for e - ver,
he may bide, he may bide with you for e - ver,

27
poco più lento
p espress. e sost.
ev'n the
ev'n the spi - rit, the
ev'n the spi - rit, the
ev'n the spi - rit, the
poco più lento
p espress. e sost.
29
rit.
spi - rit of truth, ev'n the spi - rit of truth.
spi - rit, the spi - rit of truth, the spi - rit of truth.
spi - rit of truth, ev'n the spi - rit of truth.
spi - rit the spi - rit of truth,
spi - - rit of truth, the spi - rit of truth.
rit.

*For Grupo Vocal Olisipo*

# Irish Blessing

Traditional

**BOB CHILCOTT**

Also available separately: BC18; ISBN 0-19-343229-3

© Oxford University Press 1997 and 2002. Photocopying this copyright material is ILLEGAL.

13
cresc.
mf
And un - til we meet a - gain,
cresc.
mf
17
dolce
div.
unis.
May God hold you, may God hold you, e - ver in the
mp
21
palm of his hand.
mp
25
SOPRANO
mf
ALTO
May the road rise to meet you, may the wind be e-ver at your
TENOR
BASS
mf
mf

29
back, may the sun shine warm u - pon your face, and the
32
cresc.
rain fall soft u-pon your fields, And un - til we meet a -
T. your fields,
cresc.
cresc.
36
f
dolce
mf
(div.)
S. hold you, may God
gain, may God hold you,
f
mf
f
mf

hold you,
40
mp
hold you, e - ver in the palm of his hand,
mp
mp
poco rit.
a little slower
44
p
E - ver in the palm of his hand.
p
poco rit.
a little slower
p
48
p
rit. e dim.
pp
the palm of his hand.
p
pp
rit. e dim.
pp

# Just as I am

Charlotte Elliot (1789–1871)

**BOB CHILCOTT**

Also available separately: BC6; ISBN 0-19-351149-5

© Oxford University Press 1995 and 2002. Photocopying this copyright material is ILLEGAL.

12
poco cresc.
S.
A.
many a con - flict, many a doubt, fight - ings with-in and fears with-out, O
T.
- bout with many a con-flict, many a doubt, B.
poco cresc.
poco cresc.
16
mf cresc.
f
Lamb of God, I come. Just as I am, poor, wret-ched, blind; sight,
mf cresc.
f
mf cresc.
20
mp
poco
ri-ches, heal - ing of the mind, yea, all I need, in thee to find,
mp
poco
f

24
p
O Lamb of God, I come.
p
p sonore
p sost.
29
SOPRANO p poco espress.
Just as I am, thou wilt re-ceive, wilt
ALTO p poco espress.
Just as I am, thou wilt re-ceive,
33
poco cresc.
wel-come, par - don, cleanse, re - lieve, be - cause thy pro - mise
poco cresc.
wilt wel-come, par - don, cleanse, re - lieve, be-cause thy pro - mise
poco cresc.

36
mp espress.
I be-lieve, O Lamb of God, I come. Just as I am (thy
mp espress.
I be-lieve, O Lamb of God, I come. Just as I am
TENOR & BASS (unis.)
mp espress.
Just as I
mp
40
mf
love un-known has bro-ken ev - ery bar - rier down;) now
(thy love un-known has bro-ken ev - ery bar - rier down;) now
T.
B.
am (thy love un-known has bro-ken ev - ery bar - rier down;) now
mf

43
S.
A.
T.
B.
f
to be thine, yea, thine a-lone, O Lamb of God, I come. Just as I am, of
f
f
48
mp semplice
that free love the breadth, length, depth and height to prove, here for a sea - son,
mp semplice
52
poco
p
pp
then a - bove, O Lamb of God, I
p
p sonore

* Keyboard reduction for rehearsal only.

# Song

Gerard Manley Hopkins (1844–89) **BOB CHILCOTT**

The horn part can be found on pages 50 and 51, and may be enlarged on a photocopier if required.

A slightly different arrangement of this piece can be found as the second movement of *Jubilate* by Bob Chilcott, BC26; ISBN 0-19-355827-0

© Oxford University Press 2002. Photocopying this copyright material is ILLEGAL.

11
p
What I know of thee I bless, As ac - know - ledg - ing thy stress On my
mp espress.
p
cresc.
14
be - ing and as see - ing Some - thing of thy ho - li - ness.
dim.
poco stringendo
16
mp cresc.
Once I turned from thee and hid, Bound on what thou hast for - bid;
poco stringendo
mp cresc.

18
f
sow the wind I would; I sinned: I re -
mf
f
f
rit.
a tempo
20
p
- pent of what I did.
Bad I am, but yet thy child.
p
rit.
a tempo
p

23
Fa-ther, be thou re-con-ciled. Spare thou me, since I see With thy might that thou art

poco stringendo
26
mp cresc.
mild. I have life left with me still And thy pur-pose to ful-fill;
poco stringendo
mp cresc.

29
rit.
f
dim.
Yea a debt to pay thee yet: Help me, sir, and so I will.
mf
f
rit.
dim.
f
dim.
a tempo
32
p
cresc.
But thou bidst and just thou art, Me show mer-cy from my heart To-wards my
p
cresc.
a tempo
p
cresc.
35
bro-ther, ev'-ry oth-er Man my mate and coun-ter-part, to-wards my

38
dim. e rit.
a tempo
3
p
bro - ther_ ev' - ry oth - er Man my mate and count - er - part.
dim.
p
dim. e rit.
a tempo
dim.
p
41
SOPRANO
p espress.
ALTO
Thee, God, I come from, to thee
TENOR
BASS
p espress.
pp
p
dim.
pp

45
All day
poco cresc.
go, long I like foun-tain flow From thy hand-out swayed a-bout
poco cresc.
poco cresc.
mp
48
Mote-like in thy migh-ty glow. What I know of thee I
p
p
p
mp
p

51
As ac - know-ledg-ing thy stress On my
poco cresc.
bless,
- know-ledg-ing thy stress On my be-ing and as see-ing Some-thing
poco cresc.
poco cresc.
mp
54
poco stringendo
mp cresc.
I have life left with me
of thy ho - li - ness
mp cresc.
I have life left with me still And thy pur-pose to ful-fil;
poco stringendo
mp cresc.

57
Yea a debt to
mf
f
rit.
mp
dim.
still; to pay thee yet: Help me, sir, and so I will.
f
Yea a debt to
mp
dim.
f
dim.
rit.
f
dim.
60
a tempo
p
Me show
cresc.
But thou bidst and just thou art, mer-cy from my heart To-wards my
p
cresc.
p
mp espress.
a tempo
p
p cresc.

63
dim.
bro-ther, ev'-ry oth-er Man my mate and coun-ter-part, to-wards my
dim.
dim. e rit.
a tempo
66
bro-ther, ev'-ry oth-er Man my mate and coun - ter - part.
p
dim. e rit.
a tempo
p

70
SOPRANO (or TENOR) SOLO
p
mp
Thee, God, I come from, to thee go, to thee
p
mp
Thee, God, I come from, to thee go,
p
mp
pp
pp
74
go.
go.
p
pp

*For Simon Carrington*

**HORN PART**

# Song

Gerard Manley Hopkins (1844–89)

**BOB CHILCOTT**

This and the following page may be enlarged on a photocopier if required.

© Oxford University Press 2002

40
a tempo
p
pp
44
p
poco cresc.
mp
48
p
52
poco string.
2
poco cresc.
mp
57
rit.
a tempo
f
dim.
p
61
mp espress.
65
dim. e rit.
a tempo
p
70
2
pp
75
p

*Commissioned in 2001 by The Vaulkhard Choral Trust*
*for the Choir Schools' Association*

# Sweet Prospect

Samuel Stennett (1727–95)

**BOB CHILCOTT**

Also available separately: BC53; ISBN 0-19-343303-6

© Oxford University Press 2002. Photocopying this copyright material is ILLEGAL.

12
cast a wish - ful eye, To Ca - naan's fair and
15
hap - py land, where my pos - sess - ions lie. O
18
ff
the trans - port - ing, rap - turous scene, that ri - ses to my
ff
ff

21
sight, Sweet fields ar-rayed in li-ving green, and
24
ri-vers of de-light.
f
27

31
f
O'er all those wide ex -
unis.
f
Solo reed
f
35
- tend - ed plains, shines one e - ter - nal day; There
38
God the Son for - e - ver reigns, and scat - ters night, scat - ters
and scat - ters night a -

41
SOPRANO DESCANT
ff
O the trans-port - ing, rap-turous scene, that
S.
A.
night a - way, O the trans-port - ing, rap-turous scene, that
T.
B.
- way.
(non solo)
44
ri - ses to my sight, Sweet fields ar-rayed in
ri - ses to my sight, Sweet fields ar-rayed in

47
li - ving green, and ri-vers of de - light.
li - ving green, and ri-vers of de - light.
ff
Solo Reed
51
55
ff
No
ff

58
chill - ing winds or pois - 'nous_ breath can_ reach that health - ful
(non solo)
61
shore;_ Sick - ness and sor - row, pain and_ death, are_
64
felt and feared_ no_ more. O_ the trans - port - ing,

67
rap-turous scene, that ri - ses to my sight, Sweet
70
fields ar - rayed in li - ving green, and ri - vers of de -
73
SOPRANO DESCANT
O the trans-port - ing, rap-turous scene, that
-light. O the trans-port - ing, rap-turous scene, that

76
ri - ses to my sight, Sweet fields ar-rayed in
ri - ses to my sight, Sweet fields ar-rayed in
79
fff
li - ving green, and ri-vers of de - light.
fff
li - ving green, and ri-vers of de - light.
fff
fff

*For Terry Price and the Sanctuary Choir of Preston Hollow Presbyterian Church, Dallas, Texas*

# Walk Softly

Early Shaker anthem

**BOB CHILCOTT**

© Oxford University Press 2002. Photocopying this copyright material is ILLEGAL.

12
S.
A.
T.
B.
f (with fervour!)
free, we're free from Sa-tan's bands We will walk soft - ly.
While we are
p
f (with fervour!)
f
16
pass - ing thro' the sa-cred door, In - to the fold where Christ has gone be -
19
-fore, We will walk soft - ly.
p dolce
We'll wor-ship and bow
p dolce
Solo
p

23
down we will re - joice And when we hear the Shep-herd's
26
gen - tle voice We will walk soft - ly, soft - ly,
29
mp dolce
p
poco rit.
soft - - ly, We will walk soft - - ly.
mp dolce
p
poco rit.